MW00877087

Homegrown

Our First Steps in Bringing the Church Back Home

By William T "Bill" Faris

ISBN Number: 978-1-257-62318-1

1

To my Vineyard at Home friends and family –

Thanks for risking, learning, serving, supporting and pioneering this mission and call with me. You have certainly taught me as much as I have taught you.

Love God. Love People. Repeat.

Contents

Introduction

Welcome to our church. You can park right on the street. Now pass through the gate on the white picket fence and make for the front door. Yeah, that's right: we meet in a house, not a church building. See, the door is open – come on in!

Now that you're inside you'll probably detect the smell of scrambled eggs, breakfast sausage or waffles being prepared in the kitchen. Don't worry the donuts will be arriving soon. This week, Eric brought his famous breakfast burritos. I brought some oatmeal. And, over there, you'll find some yogurt, fresh fruit and an excellent potato and ham hot dish, too. Breakfast is a little different each week because everybody brings something to share. The upshot is that none of us have a better (or more filling) breakfast all week! Would you like some coffee? Our hostess will be happy to make you a latte' upon request.

You may be wondering how long all this eating goes on before church begins. Well, it already has!

Look around you. What do you see? Family life! It's noisy. Kids are running by - laughing as they go. Teenagers are sprawled on the big couches, talking and finishing off their first helping of breakfast food. And, yes, we grownups are noisy too. Last week we were blaring out theme songs from old TV shows! Today, however, we're just swapping stories about the

4

week – moments punctuated with laughter, ooohs, aaahhhhs and a second-rate joke or two. If we sound like a family, look like a family, and act like a family it's because we *are* a family – the family of God! And, while you're with us, you're family, too.

After awhile, you'll notice several of us making our way into the living room. Before long everyone is there finding a seat. Now a guitar is being tuned and prepared for playing. Sheets with the lyrics to today's worship song selections are making the rounds. Adults and smaller children are together in the living room and little Madison, our "worship dog" is sprawled out in typical fashion in the middle of the floor.

The pre-teens and teenagers have taken seats on the stairs. Some sit way above the rest of us on the second story landing. Our meeting (what we used to call "the service" in traditional church) is about to begin!

After an opening prayer of thanksgiving and invocation, the guitarist begins his strumming and the sound of singing fills the room. After a couple praise songs, a moment of quiet follows as we wait upon the Lord. Someone spontaneously reads a few verses from the Psalms aloud. More singing follows. At the next break, someone else shares a word of encouragement they believe the Lord has inspired them to bring to our attention. Meanwhile, one of the smaller children is quietly moving wooden blocks into the outline of a cross on the carpeted floor. All in all, there is a comfortable familiarity mixed with a feeling that anything can happen.

Announcements come next. The weekend for the free neighborhood festival we are throwing is getting close. Who is manning the giant inflatable water slide? Who's got the cotton candy, slush machine, hot dogs and cold drinks covered? Who's running the cake walk? Is everything ready for the face painting, crafts, kids' games and ad hoc ping-pong tournament in the cul de sac? What about the live concert that will follow around the corner? Will the folding chairs be delivered on time? Will there be time to set up the sound system on the street?

Next, the teenagers and their adult leader remind us of their plans to hold a car wash fundraiser in a few weeks. Proceeds will be used to buy supplies for the community crisis pregnancy clinic we support. Someone else shares the good news that the large boxes of Christmas gifts we shipped to the children's home in the Philippines have arrived at last – in February! Wait 'til you see the photos of the kids opening the personalized gifts and the cards our "microchurch" kids made for them. Talk about excited! Listening, you may be amazed at the wide variety of projects and activities coming from such a small group. Believe me, so are we! But, then again, we are relatively undistracted by the other "church stuff" that used to occupy a lot of our time.

The meeting shifts to a time of Bible study and discussion. Everyone in the room reads a few verses from this week's chapter until the entire text for the week has been read out loud. What are the themes we are seeing in this scripture portion? How do we see them applying to our lives? What's that – you've got a question? Go ahead and bring it up. We actually like talking about the things that come up for people in the room. Really. We don't consider your thoughts or questions to be an interruption. We all learn from each other around here. In fact, some of the most poignant and insightful comments come from the kids.

This week, the teens are leaving the rest of us so to join their adult leader for their own Bible discussion in the backyard near the swimming pool. It's such a beautiful day outside – no wonder we like it so much in Southern California! What a shame it would be for them to have to stay cooped up inside a building when it is so nice outdoors! Next week, they'll begin fund raising for their upcoming "30 Hour Famine" for world hunger relief.

Now that our time of reading and discussing the Bible has come to an end let's see if anyone would like to receive personal prayer from the group. Don't worry; we're not in a hurry. We just want to know how we can we stand together with you in the challenges and opportunities you are facing. After all, the Bible teaches that we believers are the "Body of Christ" and "members of one another". So would you like us to pray for you? Great. Is God giving anyone specific insights to share as we move into prayer? If so, be sure and share them. Okay, let's pray while listening for what God wants us to say or do as we go. "More, Lord! Let Your kingdom come and Your will be done". Who would like to be next?

As the time for interpersonal prayer draws to a close, things are starting to wind down. One of us is already doing the dishes (our host family has enough to do on a Sunday morning to get ready for house church!). The living room is getting straightened up while one of the adults goes outside to see how the teenagers and their leader are doing. What? Some of them are in the pool already? (What do you mean they are swimming in their street clothes?!) So that's why there's so much noise and laughter all of a sudden! Man, I love the way anything can happen at our home-based "mini church"!

"What time is it", you ask? It's nearly noon. Yep, you've been here three hours since arriving for the breakfast feast. The time flies, doesn't it? Well, come on back for the neighborhood festival next Saturday. Perhaps you could take a shift at managing the line at the waterslide or cooking up a few hot dogs. This is just one way we are taking who we are together to the neighborhood. Next Spring, we'll set up another one of our outdoor Easter Sunday worship services in the open air right on the street. This summer we'll begin a Taco Tuesday Bible Study. Perhaps we'll throw another neighborhood Vacation Bible School this year or prepare another one of our in-house Christmas Eve services. This event features a home grown Nativity play staged in garage! It's not the kind of splashy holiday spectacle you'll find at larger churches but if you like your

8

Christmas simple, heartfelt, and real you can find it here. That's the house church way – at least it's the way we do house church!

* * * * * * * * * * * * * * * *

Making your way home, you review your microchurch experience. Let's see: there were no official greeters, ushers, pews, worship bands, offering baskets, lecture-styled sermons or rush for the door as the closing song was concluding. There was no appeal for the building fund and no visitor cards to fill out. Instead, you joined with other people in a hospitable home environment as they practiced loving God, each other, their neighborhood, their community and their world in ways both large and small. "Hmmmm...", you reflect. Can a microchurch be a real church, too? Read on to find out what I have begun to learn about that question.

William T "Bill" Faris, MPC - Coto de Caza, California

Chapter One

What is a Homegrown Church?

In the Introduction, I described a typical Sunday at our house church. If you are new to house churches the thought of focusing on simple things like eating together, learning from one another, reaching out together and following Christ as a "family" may intrigue you. However, the notion of making a house church community the mainstay of your Christian fellowship, worship and service may difficult to imagine. If so, statistics show you're not alone. Most American believers have not exchanged membership in a familiar, conventional church for membership in alternative type of church.

There is; however, a growing number of people who are interested in house church and other church modalities. They are not represented by any single life stage, denominational affiliation, or socio-economic background and yet they share an attraction to the simplicity, authenticity and a Christ-centered focus of a mini church. Many believers are rethinking ministry, outreach, fellowship, maturity, worship and other aspects of how God's people gather, worship, serve and inter-relate. As a result, new patterns and understandings of what it means to be the Body of Christ are emerging in our time. Perhaps you are on such a quest.

Defining House Church

If we are going to understand the microchurch / house church way of life and the philosophy of ministry that shapes it, it would be helpful to look more closely at some terminology. For the purposes of this book, I am using the terms "house church", "microchurch" and "minichurch" somewhat interchangeably. The language surrounding the rise of small, alternative, and home-based churches has been changing. The literature now references the terms "organic" church, "simple" church and "house church" and so on. It is important to note that there is no single template for all microchurches to follow. Yet, they do share some common characteristics. We'll list some of these in a moment, but for now let's take a look at how the term "house church" has been used in the contemporary literature. We're starting here because "house church" is the granddaddy term and the one that covers the most ground in describing alternative microchurches so far.

The house church movement in the West and around the world has been examined by a wide range of missiologists, researchers, academics and practitioners for some time now. Prominent church researcher George Barna is among those who have attempted to survey the contemporary church landscape including the traditional church and alternative church communities of faith. In 2007, Mr. Barna and his research team published the results of a survey that focused on the rise of house churches in the U.S. In this survey, a "house church" was described as:

"...a group of believers that meets regularly in a home or place other than a church building. These groups are not part of a typical church; they meet independently, are self-governed and consider themselves to be a complete church on their own... (They are) sometimes known as a house church or simple church, (and are) not associated in any way with a local, congregational type of church."(1).

Authors Robert and Julia Banks have their own definition for "home church" in their book *The Church Comes Home*. They see home church as "a kind of extended Christian family that involves singles, married (couples), and their children" who:

"...meet regularly to develop communally a shared Christian life, to relate each member's faith to everyday life, and to deepen each member's relationship with God. They may meet in a house, a condominium or an apartment – wherever "home" is for the members of the group and wherever they feel most "at home". (2)

The Banks' then distinguish stand-alone home churches from "home church-based-congregations" or networks. These networks are "a group or cluster of independent house churches that meet together regularly and have some common objectives". (3)

One of the key features of house churches is their emphasis on the direct headship of Christ. House churches tend to eschew or even openly reject the notion of leadership that is vested in denominationally appointed or professionally trained pastoral leaders or clergy. In his book *Houses that Change the World,* author Wolfgang Simson notes that "the house church is a way of living the Christian life communally in ordinary homes through supernatural power. It is the way redeemed people live locally. It is the organic way disciples follow Jesus together in everyday life."(4)

Southern Baptist author and researcher J.D. Payne picks up this theme when he writes that, although small in size, a house church tends to "consider itself fully autonomous, meaning that, under the headship of Christ and the Word, the church makes its own decisions regarding plans, strategies, purchases, leadership, worship expressions, missions and so on" (5)

Here, then, are some of the key themes I have found in house church literature:

- Everyday people meeting in houses or other kinds of everyday settings as the mainstay of their participation in Christian community
- A simple focus on actualizing the basics of The Faith as opposed to the implementation of highly-developed church programming
- Participation of the total house church membership in decision making, spiritual direction, and the practice of The Faith

- Group roles shaped by individual gifts and abilities rather than officially bestowed ministerial titles or professional training
- Accountability that is localized and Christ-centered rather than denominationally rooted or trans-local
- An effort to organize around the timeless and "organic" elements of church life and mission rather than traditions, trends, or particular personalities.

Church Lite?

As I noted earlier, the research confirms that most American Christians continue to identify with a conventional local church as their home base for faith development, worship and service. However, a quest for simplicity, authenticity, and organic Christianity is beginning to express itself in new ways across the American church landscape. Little by little, the grip of conventional church modalities on the imagination of American believers is loosening. As a result, the notion of bringing church home is beginning to become more acceptable.

George Barna identifies this trend when he notes that "the ideas of worshipping in homes rather than church buildings, and being led by group members rather than religious professionals, are new to most Americans... many people are just beginning to think about, and get comfortable with, the idea of homes being the dominant place for shared faith experiences". (5)

14

While this may represent a new phenomenon to Western believers, it is important to remember that in other parts of the world house churches are not only common but, in some localities, they are the predominant expression of lively Christian community. (6)

Unfortunately, a stubborn "edifice complex" continues to influence conventional church life in the United States where bigger is usually assumed to be better. Church growth, as measured in attendance figures, involvement in church programs and financial abundance is often treated as a de facto sign of God's blessing and affirmation by both church leaders and members. The notion of the local church building as "God's House" is still not hard to find where traditional church thinking rules. Therefore, the concept of living out one's faith in the deconstructed community of a microchurch may seem to be little more than a second-rate substitute of the real thing – a sort of "church lite".

It's not hard understand this when, historically, church buildings have functioned as religiously consecrated spaces set apart to fulfill important roles in a given community. The local church campus has traditionally been the place where people worship, learn about God, adopt a particular faith system, solemnize their wedding vows, go to Sunday school, and attend the funerals or memorial services of their loved ones. For this reason, many people find it difficult to conceive of living without the conventional church at the center of their spiritual life. After all, many features of big church cannot successfully be shrunken down to miniature.

Therefore, if one is going to truly adopt the house church as their mainstay faith community, it will require a profound and fundamental shift away from some of the deeply embedded traditional paradigms of church life, leadership, mission and makeup. For those coming from a more traditional church background, these shifts can be more than a little daunting!

My hope is that by sharing my own experiences of embracing the microchurch way of life, assistance and encouragement will be made available to others interested in seeing what God is doing in the alternative mini-church movements of our time. Be informed that it is not my intention to deliver a scholarly study of alternative church movements or a full-fledged *apologia* for innovative new church communities. Instead, I am seeking to share what I know with those who are just curious or who are considering taking the plunge for themselves.

I have spent a lifetime in conventional evangelical churches as a pastor, leader, and member. Because of this, I know the traditional, mainstream church backwards and forwards. Therefore, let me make it clear that I am not "anti" (traditional) church. Indeed, I regularly speak in local churches and provide professional counseling and other kinds of support to pastors, church members and leaders from these church backgrounds. I have friends and family members who are involved professionally and non-professionally in mainstream churches and I care deeply about their lives and ministries. I am aware that this sets me apart from some of those who see house church / simple church / organic church as the only authentic expressions of the church as conceived by Jesus and the Apostles.

Although I do not share this point of view, I have come to enthusiastically and unapologetically embrace microchurch Christianity. I love the elegant simplicity of this form of church life. But, more importantly, I deeply appreciate the way my house church involvement allows me to experience the Person of Jesus Christ, His community and His mission in my own life and in the lives of others. Having tasted microchurch Christianity for myself, I am firm in my conviction that *it is a wholly legitimate way to reach people for Christ, encourage spiritual maturity in believers, serve the needs of the community, and glorify God.*

In the next chapter, I will take you into my own transformation from a professionally trained and experienced pastor in full-time local church ministry to a "house church guy". It is not a story of regret or revolution. Rather, it is one man's "extreme makeover" as a contemporary Christ-follower who has continued to follow wherever He leads.

(1) http://www.barna.org/barna-update/article/19-organic-church/112-house-churches-are-more-satisfying-to-attenders-than-are-conventional-churches, viewed May 17, 2010

(2) Banks, Robert & Julia, *The Church Comes Home*, Peabody, MA, Hendrickson Publishers Inc, 1998, p. vii

(3) Simson, Wolfgang, *Houses that Change the World,* Carlisle, Cumbria, Canada, OM Publishing, 1998, p. 79

(4) Payne, J.D., *Missional House Churches,* Colorado Springs, CO, Paternoster Publishers, 2008, p. 13

(5) Barna, ibid

(6) For an excellent eyewitness account of one indigenous man's experience of the house church in mainland China, see the book *The Heavenly Man,* by Brother Yun with Paul Hattaway.

Chapter Two

My Story

"You have to let me go".

I was surprised to hear myself say those words to our congregation during that final Sunday night "family meeting" of the Crown Valley Vineyard Church. I had no plans to say any such thing. The words, having undeniably come from my mouth, seemed to hang in the air over my head. Yes, these dear people would have to let me go. For years I had been their pastor and, in many ways, they had become family to me and one other. Our bonds had been forged working side-by-side to plant a new Vineyard church in Southern California. And now, eight years following our launch, it was time to close down the church as we knew it. Moving on to the things God had been preparing for each of us would require us to let go of a very precious and familiar life style in order to allow new ground to be broken.

Over the course of the months preceding the wrap up of our traditional church, I had been developing some big new ideas about my own next steps. This new direction was being shaped by a comprehensive season of reading, prayer, personal assessment, reflection and counseling with mentors. As a result, my imagination was beginning to be unleashed and a new vision was taking shape within me. I had finally come to the point of admitting that my original mission to successfully plant a conventional Vineyard church had become unsustainable. It was time to take a bold new course. God willing, this new endeavor would result in a network of microchurches or, as they are more commonly known, house churches.

Despite my conviction that God was leading me to move out in this direction, anxieties abounded. Some of these uncomfortable feelings were rooted in the very understandable "why?" questions that came from the people around me. After all, I had earned their respect as a Christian leader but the shift I was embracing raised many more questions than I could answer. The adventurous among us were intrigued and even excited. But others were confused and, perhaps, a little angry. Nevertheless, I felt certain that this new direction was necessary and timely. I was aware that some or even most of our present congregation would not be ready to follow me into this change and I wanted to help them get into another church body where they could thrive. There were others, however, who let me know that they were ready for the adventure of exploring life as a house church. In the end, everyone wound up in the place for which they felt best suited.

When the day of the final Sunday morning worship service of the Crown Valley Vineyard arrived in July, 2008 we came together to celebrate all God had done in our lives through this wonderful church. There was a big pancake breakfast, tears, laughter, memories, flowers, awards, a video retrospective and more. At the end of the service I presented a small bottle of perfume to each person in attendance. The perfume was to serve as a reminder of our call and commission to take the sweet spiritual fragrance of what we had experienced together at CVV into our future. Our future ministries, churches and friendships would certainly be enriched by all the wonderful things God had done in our lives over the time we had spent together. The bottles of fragrance symbolized our desire to pour out the blessings we had received as an offering to God and for the benefit of others.

A Church Triumphant

For me, this goodbye was tremendously bittersweet. To that point, I had never been more committed to anything than I had been to leading and serving in the Crown Valley Vineyard Church. Our church had initially been planted in the opening months of the year 2000. It was not only the first year of a new century but it was also the start of a new millennium. Our hopes were high that this new church would bloom and grow in that amazing season of new beginnings! Right away, however, my family and our entire church planting team were hit with an unexpected tragedy. Four days after being sent out by our home church to begin our new mission my wife and two of our four children were involved in a head-on automobile collision.

Robin had been driving the kids home from school on that rain-soaked afternoon when a pickup truck lost control and crossed the center line into her path. The children did not suffer any serious injuries but Robin was brutally hurt in the crash. That she survived the accident at all was remarkable. That she eventually recovered from brain injury and dozens of fractured bones was a miracle. Nevertheless, Robin's recovery would require months of hospitalization, surgeries, physical therapy and other intensive interventions. All sense of normalcy in our lives had been swallowed up by the many and varied tasks of recovery.

As our family fought our way back from the tragedy that had befallen us we couldn't help but wonder what would happen to our dream of planting the new church? Would our mission go forward or would it be permanently derailed? To our amazement, the startup team for the new church redoubled their efforts to stay the course and launch the new work. Looking back, it seems the crash somehow increased our resolve to successfully establish the church despite the obstacles we faced. As a result, The Crown Valley Vineyard began holding regular Sunday services in the summer of 2000 – just a few months after the accident. It was a church that had been born in a time of pain, fire, love, vision and determination. Perhaps that is why God used it to bring strength, healing and renewal to so many over the years that followed.

For three years our new congregation met in rented school facilities. Then we were presented with an opportunity to sign a five year lease on 5,400 square feet of church space that was about to become available in the heart of our community. The accommodations were not particularly large or impressive but it felt like a real step up to us. Before long we were signing papers and preparing to move in. Our imaginations were overflowing with visions of the exciting and effective new ministries we could launch from our new home base. Sure, the financial commitment would be daunting but we felt confident that our attendance would soon grow to the level where we could more easily manage the commitments we were making. After years of loading and unloading trailers and setting up in temporary rented space it seemed as if the time was ripe for us to become a "real church" at last!

Four years later, our decision to take on the building was proving to be painful. The price of our lease had climbed to nearly $9,000 per month and yet our congregation had never grown in overall size. We had started the church with less than one hundred adults in 2000. Seven years later, we still had about the same number in attendance. Although our people were faithful givers, our expenses far surpassed our income. We were running as "lean and mean" as we could and yet we were virtually bleeding money. We depended upon funds drawn from our once impressive reserves to remain operational while we worked, hoped and prayed for a breakthrough to come at last. But with the clock ticking and no change in sight, our moment of truth as a congregation had arrived.

There was simply no way to continue the course we were on. This left us with some important questions. Should we relocate and share church space with another congregation? Should we go back to meeting in a school? Or was it time to take an altogether different course? Decisions needed to be made.

Asking Questions

Over the years I have observed that crisis has a way of causing us to ask questions we might otherwise ignore. As I faced the compelling issues related to the future of our church, one particular question repeated in my mind: *"what would you do if you didn't do what you've always done?"* This was an intriguing new question, indeed. For eight years I had been obsessed with the question of: *"what will it take to get this church to move up to the next level of growth and impact?"* We surveyed our members, fine-tuned our programs, and prayed with passion. Despite our efforts, the "high impact" (or even steady growth) we were seeking continued to elude us. How could a loving, active, welcoming church that was located in a fast-growing part of our county find it so difficult to grow? What was it that was keeping us from reaching deeper into our community? Why were we locked in a holding pattern we could no longer afford to sustain? Was this really all God had in mind for our church and our mission? Slowly, a new way of thinking began to present itself. Perhaps God was actually trying to speak to us through our situation. Perhaps He was inviting me to see ministry, church life and mission form a totally different perspective. Perhaps this was the story HE was writing about our church.

As a lifelong ministry professional I have learned a lot about Christian leadership, mission, personal growth, corporate growth and church life over the years. I had been serving on the staff of both large and small churches since I was in my twenties. But now I felt strangely as if I was a new beginner. Why? Had things changed so much that I somehow "missed the boat"? Perhaps. But a better explanation seemed to be that God was calling me to a cutting edge. This was confirmed to me when a respected friend shared a spiritual impression he had received during a dinner meeting. "A few minutes ago I got these words in my mind and I think they were from the Lord: 'Bill is finally getting out of the mushy middle'". Is that what this was about?

To know for certain would require further soul-searching and exploration. Could I find the courage to embrace such a call at this time in my life? Would I be willing to investigate new ideas about church leadership, fellowship, structure and mission even if it meant "starting over"? The choices were getting clearer.

Around this time I began to reflect on something I learned from Vineyard leader John Wimber; one of my key "fathers in the faith". In speaking of his own remarkable spiritual journey, John revisited the familiar parable of Jesus commonly referred to as "The Pearl of Great Price" (Matthew 13: 34, 35). In discussing the text, he pointed out that Jesus meant for this to be a parable of the kingdom of God (see verse 34). In other words, John said, it was one of the ways Christ was describing what it was like to be under the rule and reign of God. It was not, he emphasized, only a way of describing our initial surrender in salvation. Rather, it was Jesus' way of describing the ongoing choices that make up the life of a continually growing believer.

In the story, the merchant was in fact a pearl *trader* and not a pearl *collector*. His reason for selling everything in order to buy the pearl had to do with his intention to later re-sell it for a profit. That's what pearl merchants do! In applying the lesson of the parable to our lives, John described how those who continually seek God's kingdom in their lives will come to a point, time and again, when they will be faced with the need to "sell all" in order to obtain the thing of greater value in their walk with God. This, he said, was his own experience and we should not be surprised if it is ours as well. Something about John's interpretation of the words of Jesus fit my situation well and gave me the feeling that I was finally beginning to understand what was happening in my life.

As I read, prayed, thought and processed the things I was learning, I began to grow more excited by a new vision of ministry that was beginning to develop. The thought of deconstructing the unsustainable situation we were in was both daunting and exciting. While it would be bittersweet to bring the efforts we had made to plant our church in the traditional manner to an end; I could see that doing so would allow some of us to launch into an entirely new direction. The kind of church I was now starting to envision combined some of the timeless features of the New Testament church with a contemporary and "cutting edge" approach to church life and mission. It would emphasize simplicity in the way we would meet from house-to-house and seek to take ministry directly to the neighborhood level by empowering everyday people to serve and worship God. Yet, it would also have an "all together" touch point which would allow us to reinforce our identity as part of a greater whole.

At that time, I was beginning to get acquainted with contemporary thinking about networks, decentralized educational, business and social structures, and some of the more "organic" approaches to church life. The more I learned, the more I began to reframe the exciting possibilities of leading a network of microchurches. My excitement about the possibilities increased.

These various explorations were leading me into a total paradigm shift. What if our church no longer chose to spend our resources on a building or on hiring staff? What if we utilized homes and other everyday places instead? What if we let go of the traditional church planting goal of building up a single central campus and shifted instead to the creation of a network of mini-churches that would occasionally meet "all together" in borrowed or rented space? What if we shifted from the idea of getting people to come to church (so we could do ministry to them) to the idea of taking the church to the people through the natural relationships that already existed? What if we redistributed our donation money so that a portion of it would be regularly returned to the givers via their house churches? In this way, they would become responsible as a microchurch "on the ground" to determine how God wanted them to spend these funds on their mission for Him. Wow. Imagine a church that would actually give money back to the givers and beg them to figure out how God wanted them to spend it!

As it developed, my new "microchurch" thinking represented the flip side of the attractional church growth model. This approach to church growth and discipleship has dominated the evangelical church for the past generation and has, in part, produced the phenomenon of the megachurch. The attractional church growth model utilizes the engaging power of first-rate worship services, finely-tuned programs and special events so as to attract potential new believers and church members to the "mothership" (the church campus) where invitees come within range of professional ministry of various kinds. The attractional approach tends to operate on the assumption that "bigger is better."

This ministry paradigm has redefined many of the historic roles and expectations placed upon pastors and other ministry professionals in our times. The attractional philosophy of ministry has also transformed the look of church facilities, the sounds and styles of church music, the quality of church communication techniques, and the overall level of reliance upon technology that runs through the church. Even the style of church teaching and preaching has been impacted by attraction-based ministry as have the nature of the appeals made to newcomers and established church members alike.

Under the attractional paradigm, church members are consistently encouraged to be "inviters and includers" who bring their friends and family with them to church services, outreaches, and events. Those who come within range of the church's influence are considered to be a part of the "crowd" constituency. Under the attractional model, efforts are made to systematically engage members of the crowd with the message of Christ and then move them through the requirements that will qualify them to take their place among the church's more "committed" members. The end game is for these committed members to eventually become a full-fledged part of the congregation's "core".

In contrast to this approach, the microchurch / house church paradigm offers "visitors" or "newcomers" immediate access to core members. This access and inclusion *is* the attraction factor of the microchurch. It may be helpful to think of the contrast between a chain restaurant, store or hotel versus a "mom and pop" eatery, specialty store, or bed and breakfast inn that is run by the establishment's owners. House church / microchurch offers a "high touch / low tech" means of creating relationship and belonging as compared to the attractional church's "high tech / low touch" multi-layered approach.

Our situation would not allow us much time to slowly introduce a shift to a house church network or some sort of "hybrid" situation. Instead, embracing a shift to a house church network would require us to deconstruct our local church as we knew it. Our people would need to "let me go" from the familiar roles I had played in their lives and I would need to "let them go", too. This parting of the ways would be the first in a series of difficult but necessary makeovers that would redefine our ministry, church life, and mission. In the next chapter, I will describe the transformation that accomplished this comprehensive redefinition.

Chapter Three

Underway

There it was – that nagging word. It had been popping into my head over the weekend and now, on Tuesday morning, it was on my mind again. *Skunkworks*. Such a funny word. I'd heard it before but I couldn't remember where or when. But that morning, as I slid my key into the door of the church office, an inner voice kept urging me: "Don't forget *skunkworks*". "Okay," I thought to myself. "Noted". And with that, I proceeded inside to take on the day's responsibilities.

As lunch time approached I realized that I was getting through my work rather quickly. Great. That meant I could take my lunch out in Silverado Canyon. It's about a twenty minute drive to get out to the Canyon, but for over twenty years it has been my favorite local getaway. This little township provides such a welcome alternative to the typical Orange County glitz and buzz. Without a doubt, Silverado folk enjoy a way of life that is rooted in another time and moves at another pace. At the little Silverado Café, locals gather to shoot the breeze, get a bite to eat, and drink coffee out of their own cup. Once they leave, their cup will be washed and hung up on the wall. That way it can be used to serve other customers until its owner comes back for another meal at their "home away from home".

As lunchtime approached, I was winding my way down the two lane road that leads to Silverado's simple town center. I have always found it relaxing to allow the rugged beauty of the canyon to swallow up my worries and cares. It is as if they hop out of the car at the head of Silverado Canyon Road to await my return to town. In other words, for me, Silverado is a magical place. I would soon find out that it was even more "magical" than I had previously imagined!

For a while I had been torn between the excitement of the new ministry vision that was building within me and my concerns for the people I had pastored for the past eight years and the church we had planted together. Should I really close down the Crown Valley Vineyard as such? Was this really what God wanted me to do? Although I didn't feel that I was coming at this radical change in a manner that was impulsive it still gave me pause. This was new ground that I would be breaking. Even my peers would have a hard time understanding it. Would my wife and family be okay? Would I be able to successfully replace a full-time ministry income? These were some of my ongoing questions and concerns. But that day, as I walked through the door of the Silverado Café, the only thing that was on my mind was the fact that I had already decided to (uncharacteristically) order breakfast for lunch.

I found a booth and took in the funky, familiar Café environment. When the server asked me for my order, I told him to please bring me an omelet along with some toast and a cup of coffee. While I waited, I decided to make a little more progress in a book I was reading. I was still engrossed in the book when the young waiter showed up with my coffee. "Watch the airplane disappear", he said as he plopped the steaming mug on the table next to me. Looking up, I noticed the silhouette of an airplane on the large cup. It was made out of a heat-sensitive material that dimmed and went clear as the hot coffee warmed the mug up. "Cute", I thought to myself as I returned to my reading.

Once my meal arrived, I picked up my coffee for another swallow before diving in. "I wonder what's on the other side of this mug", I thought to myself as I spun it around on the table. What I saw nearly took my breath away. There on the other side of the disappearing airplane mug was a cartoon drawing of a skunk. Above it was a single word: *Skunkworks*. Suddenly and without warning, my casual "breakfast-for-lunch" experience had turned into an impossibly cosmic communication from God.

As I stared at the mug I began to chuckle out loud. "Okay, Lord", I whispered to the One who had suddenly made Himself quite present to me. "Message received". But I still did not know the meaning of that word. Returning home, I got home I got out my laptop computer and began a word search on *Skunkworks*. The history of the word began to give me further clues about its new meaning for me. The term *Skunkworks* was originally coined to describe a collection of designers and engineers known as the Lockheed Martin Advanced Development Projects group. This incredible design team, first assembled during WWII, continued to

33

generate projects as groundbreaking as the U-2 spy plane, the SR-71 "Blackbird" jet, and a number of other highly innovative aircraft projects.

The online article went on to note that, since its origins at Lockheed, the term *Skunkworks* has come to be adopted by other corporations and institutions: *"to describe a group within an organization given a high degree of autonomy and unhampered by bureaucracy, tasked with working on advanced or secret projects"*. (1) Was God telling me that He has a *Skunkworks* of His own? Was He somehow calling me to dare to leave my familiar church practices and patterns behind in order to innovate "unhampered by bureaucracy"? Things were definitely getting interesting, that's for sure. And the mug? Well you better believe that I bought it from the Silverado Canyon resident who owned it so I could take it home to keep!

First Steps

Over the weeks that followed, I continued to move our leaders and congregation into the total transformation of our lives as a church. There had been meetings, teachings, sermons, book recommendations and many personal conversations to prepare for our shift. But the practical details of exiting our lease obligations and thinning our belongings would be daunting. The answer to our need came one day over lunch when a pastor friend of mine told me that their congregation could really use church space like ours. We followed up that conversation by putting together a space swap that would benefit both churches. They would move out of the high school space they rented each Sunday in to our dedicated church space and write a new lease with our landlord. This allowed us to take an early termination on our lease (a big relief). They also agreed to buy our chairs other "church stuff" to use in their new space. In return, we committed to sublease their rented office space for six months which freed them to move. It was a classic win-win arrangement.

Now that we were "in flight", it was time to take some next steps towards launching a house church network. We began by holding a series of Sunday night training and prayer meetings in our newly rented office space. This gave us a way to meet together, pray, teach and prepare ourselves as we plunged into the first phase of the transition. It was unfamiliar and a little awkward to function in this "in between" manner as a church. For one thing, at least half of our Crown Valley Vineyard congregation had moved on to find new church homes by that time. Those of us that remained were still feeling our way forward into a simple church modality one step at a time. It was clear that we were going to need to give ourselves time to shift mentally and emotionally from what we had always known into our new formation.

A host of practical questions remained. How should we format ministry to children and teenagers? How shall we structure our eldership and leadership as a house church network? In what ways would we need to fine-tune our philosophy of ministry and engage our mission differently as a body of believers? We decided to give ourselves six months to work these things out. At that time we would need to move out of the subleased office space and complete our church transition.

Of course, I had my own questions and concerns. What should I do about a salary now that I would no longer serve as a typical local church pastor, per se? All my life, I had been a full time paid ministry professional. I would now need to develop multiple income streams to replace my salary. And then there was the question of office space and personnel. Should we find a new space for our network to use as our "headquarters"? Should we retain our part-time administrator? What about our non-profit corporate status? Should we hold on to it? Let it go? Readjust it?

Over the weeks that followed we attempted to take on these issues and a hundred others like them. I was reminded of an advertisement I once saw which depicted a jet airliner being built while it was in flight. Yes, we had plenty of challenges to tackle as we continued to downsize, simplify and redesign our ministry and fellowship. I could only hope and pray that those who started into this adventure with us would be able to survive the shock of transition and tap into grace as we worked to see our dreams come true.

While busy leading our church family into new things "on the fly," I was also doing my best to help my own family through the changes at hand. Robin, a gifted nurse, was in a graduate school program and working in the hospital. Admittedly, I was the one initiating the church shift while my family was more or less along for the ride. In the back of my mind, I knew I was spending their trust in me as a husband, a father and a pastor and that I needed to be careful to not overstrain our family system. Of our four children, two were still at home. Matthew had recently turned fifteen and JeanneAnn was about to turn eleven. They both had grown up most of their lives in the traditional local church environment at Crown Valley Vineyard. Now, the landscape of their church experience was being altered for reasons I'm sure they could not easily grasp. But, we were committed now, and there was only one direction for us to take and that was forward into the adventure to which God was calling us.

Financial Structure

Our new philosophy of ministry required an appropriately new approach to our church's financial structure. From the beginning, we envisioned a situation in which the majority of funds contributed to our Network could be utilized for actual ministry rather than for salary compensations, building expenses and so on. Over the first eight months of our transition I continued to draw a severance equal to the salary and housing I received as the pastor of the Crown Valley Vineyard. My initial hope was to develop a sufficient number of alternative income streams to completely replace any church-sourced compensation for my leadership. And so the clock was ticking.

A big part of this need could be met if I could successfully develop a thriving practice as a professional pastoral counselor with *Marriage and Family Matters*, a local Christian counseling group. By the end of 2008, I was beginning to schedule appointments with counselees while continuing to lead our Network further into its ramp up phase. Each step forward reminded me of the way that Indiana Jones – fictional movie hero, adventurer and treasure-seeker – was required to reach his foot out into thin air and step into "nothing" before the next invisible step across a treacherous canyon would materialize. Perhaps this was the way of life the Apostle Paul had in mind when he made his inspired observation that "we walk by faith, not by sight". This way of life whereby I follow the Spirit's lead "one step at a time" has continued ever since.

Testing Prototypes

By the end of the year, a group had begun meeting in a private home in the suburban community of Foothill Ranch. Two other microchurch groups in other neighborhoods would soon follow. It felt good to me that we had something to show for all our efforts even if we still were not entirely clear on some key details. I was quickly learning that, while our core philosophy of ministry was sound, the details of microchurch life, leadership and mission would take more testing in the real world than I had at first imagined. One such detail had to do with house church leadership, eldership and oversight. I had initially envisioned a sort "circuit rider" role for myself in our Network whereby I would regularly visit each microchurch. This would allow me to see for myself how things were going, provide problem solving as needed, act as guest teacher, and supply a measure of spiritual direction. Although this seemed like a good plan in theory, I found it difficult to maintain in practice. And besides, if our dreams of one planting dozens of microchurches would one day come true it would be impossible for me to be personally present to each one.

Unfortunately, one of our original house churches (not Foothill Ranch) was formed with the expectation that I would be more present and involved than I was truly able to be. Indeed, I was the one who had set them up to expect more "hands-on" leadership from me. In addition to hosting the group in their home, it was necessary for the lead couple to provide an overall leadership role as well as to occasionally lead worship. At first the group thrived nicely. As time went on; however, a variety of factors began to undermine the survival of this house church and it was eventually closed down. Although the loss was deeply felt, the experiences of this church revealed some of the flaws as well as some of the strengths in our original vision. I will reflect on some of these lessons learned in a later chapter.

Back to Foothill Ranch

Meanwhile, the church at Foothill Ranch was thriving. This microchurch included adults, teens and children. Outwardly focused from the beginning, the members heartily embraced a mission to the surrounding neighborhood and beyond. At the time of this writing, this church has been meeting for less than two years and yet it has already:

- Sponsored two outdoor neighborhood festivals run by house church members for the benefit of the surrounding neighborhood. These free events included food, games, a bounce house or water slide attraction, face painting, a cake walk, crafts and other simple and fun-filled activities. One of these festivals concluded in an outdoor Christian music concert as well.

- Held two "home grown" Christmas Eve services which featured a Christmas-themed play (staged in the garage!), a Christmas-themed message from God's word, a time for people to openly share what Christmas means to them, carol singing and candle lighting.

- Hosted two Easter Sunday Morning outdoor worship services held on the street just around the corner from the microchurch host home. These events featured live worship music, communion, an Easter message from God's word and a hospitality time outside the host home.

- Supported the youth in a "30 Hour Famine" to benefit a world hunger program. House church youth have also held a free car wash to benefit a local crisis pregnancy clinic. They have prepared, served and cleaned up over 300 meals at a local homeless ministry, camped at the beach, reached out at a local convalescent home, developed their own monthly cycles of teaching, fellowship and leadership and fully participated in all other house church activities and events.

- Bought, wrapped and sent Christmas gifts to the Arms of Love home in the Philippines, provided gift cards to new parents through a local crisis pregnancy clinic, and held a dessert potluck to invite neighbors and friends into further contact with the house church members.

- Conducted a "homegrown" Vacation Bible School over Spring Break.

- Moved Sunday morning worship time down the street in order to share it with an elderly shut-in.

- Provided a customized basket full of gifts for a neighbor battling cancer. The basket was delivered by the entire house church which then gathered around the cancer patient and her family and laid hands on them in prayer.

This list is not exhaustive, but it does illustrate the nature of the Foothill Ranch House Church as a fully-functioning body of believers that is highly engaged in its mission to glorify God, build up believers and truly engage the unreached in the neighborhood, community and around the world.

Without Walls

The third of the original groups in our Network has its own unique shape and style. "Without Walls" (the name chosen by the group for themselves) is anchored by two couples – one in their 60's and one in their 30's.

At the time Without Walls began meeting, different people who were important to the group happened to be moving out of the area. Because Without Walls members believe that their connection to the people God has put in their lives should not be limited by geography, they sought to provide continuity of relationship to those who were relocating. That way, the people who were moving could still have "family" around them while they worked on establishing new roots in their new communities. In less than two years members of this house church have also:

- Given a sizeable amount of financial aid to people facing overwhelming medical expenses and other crises.

- Developed a remarkable network of young mothers throughout Orange County.

- Encouraged and supported group members in their ministries to the broader community (for example, one group member speaks regularly at luncheons hosted by a ministry that reaches out to women).

And so the Network was begun with three different microchurches – each with their own very different core constituencies. Each group was free to choose its own meeting schedule and style. Each house church found its own way of responding to our common mission to "empower everyday people to take the ministry of Jesus to everyday places". Each had its own stories to tell of successes, challenges, blessings and stumbling blocks. Somehow, the Vineyard Community Mission Network was underway. Rough around the edges? Yes. But refinements began almost immediately and continue to the present. In the next chapter, I will share some of the things that have turned out to be of key importance.

1. http://en.wikipedia.org/wiki/Skunk_Works, retrieved June 30, 2010.

Chapter Four

Essentials

I have come to see that the core genius of the house church / microchurch / organic church is *simplicity*. It is the simplicity of simple churches that allows them to be highly focused, reproducible, adaptable, interpersonal and truly missional. In my experience, these qualities stand in sharp contrast to the trends which push contemporary conventional churches to become more complicated, sophisticated and brand-focused. Instead of shunning simplicity; microchurches embrace it. By doing so, they maximize the spiritual gifts, resources, relationships and potential participation of every member. Experiencing this has been one of my greatest joys and one of the most refreshing discoveries I have made since focusing on homegrown church life.

Because they are not all cut from the same cloth, various microchurches tap into their possibilities in different ways. Some become strongly focused on serving particular neighborhoods, individuals or people groups in focused outreach. Others seek take so-called "Body Life" (member participation in leadership, meetings, interpersonal care and outreach) to high levels. Even those house churches that are connected to a conventional "Mother Church" find ways to take advantage of the possibilities their relative simplicity affords. This includes the opportunity to directly engage individual members in a manner that larger congregations simply cannot duplicate.

Simplicity, then, is one of the essentials ingredients of a thriving microchurch. Other essentials include:

- adaptability
- the empowerment of the total membership
- a missional focus
- a Christ-centered ethos

Adaptability

These days; the ability of institutions, businesses and service providers to become highly flexible and adaptable may well define the critical difference between those that will have a future and those that will not. It is no secret that societal, financial and political changes – and even upheaval – are common characteristics of the times in which we live. A trendy word for this potential adaptability of systems and institutions is *fluidity*. In contrast to more static systems, a fluid system is capable of flexing with change while retaining its core focus and mission.

Over the centuries, the Church of Jesus Christ has proven to be one of the world's most profoundly adaptable and fluid systems! Like two divinely-empowered batteries, the Great Commission (Matthew 28: 18-20) and the Great Commandment (Luke 10: 27) have propelled the Church forward into her mission for over 2,000 years. Despite the sometimes horrifying rigidity of the most visible expressions of the historic institutional Church; the evidence shows that the true

Church of God through the ages has demonstrated an amazing ability to survive political, social, financial and cultural upheaval while still retaining its grasp on its core witness and sources of empowerment. Anabaptists, Reformers, "High Church" believers, Pentecostal "holy rollers", Monks, Missionaries and Methodists have all produced fruit that proceeds from the two primary instincts of the Great Commission and the Great Commandment. **"For in Christ Jesus neither circumcision nor uncircumcision has any value.** *The only thing that counts is faith expressing itself through love"* **(Galatians 5: 6).**

The challenge of our times is for us as believers to be *heavy* in our core convictions while remaining *light* on our feet. Adapting to the spirit of the age has led too much of the contemporary church to get this completely backwards. Seeking institutional survival has led many churches to shed historic core convictions while maintaining traditional appearances. This has resulted in a score of denominations that are "Christian" in name only. Foreseeing this, the Apostle cautioned believers to avoid being deceived by those who **"will act as if they are religious, but they will reject the power that could make them godly"** before adding that we must **"stay away from people like that"** (II Timothy 3: 5, NLT).

The Bible reminds us that there is such a thing as **"the Faith that was once for all entrusted to the saints"** (Jude 1: 3, NIV). This unchanging Faith has proven its power to adapt to a tremendously wide variety of social, political and cultural environments. For example, I was raised in a middle class American home that identified with a liturgical form of Christianity. However, as a teenager I discovered the liberating vitality of "born again" Christianity during the so-called Jesus People Movement phenomenon within American Christianity. Over the forty years that have followed my teenage spiritual awakening, I have shared the essentials of my faith with Spirit-filled Roman Catholics in Southern California, Pentecostal believers in Arizona, "Charismatics" in Montana, "Third Wave" believers in New Zealand, renewed Anglicans in England and exuberant house church believers in China.

Over the course of my lifetime I have worshipped in cathedrals, in living rooms and in the Great Outdoors. I have been shut in tightly with Chinese house church believers in secret gatherings and I have worshipped openly with hundreds of thousands of fellow believers on the grounds of the Capitol Mall in Washington, D.C. I have praised God and sought Him heartily in school settings, industrial tilt-up buildings, New England styled church structures, great stadiums, hospital chapels and a variety of other environments.

After all this, I can make the following observation with certainty: *no religiously consecrated space has had the power to define my faith, my relationship with God, or my kinship with others just because that space is called a "church" for it is not the physical setting that gives faith its wings.* Rather, it is the power of the Holy Spirit in the life of each believer and at work in the community of faith that bears witness to the true presence of God in the Church.

I therefore feel somewhat sad and confused when I observe some of my fellow believers pouring huge amounts of money and resources into their buildings and other physical features of their dedicated church environments. Surely they understand the fact that the kingdom of God can break into even the most rudimentary environment *if* He is whole-heartedly welcomed there. Chinese house church leader, Brother Yun, author of the book *The Heavenly Man*, certainly took note of this while visiting the West for the first time when he noted that "you seem to do little with so much; while we do much with so little". Ouch.

The point here is not to slam buildings or budgets wholesale. Rather, it is to recognize that the essential life of the church is not defined by – or limited to – any particular environment. The genius of the gospel is its ability to create redemption and lift wherever believers gather in the glorious Name of Jesus, adopt His mission, teach His Word and worship His majesty. This is why microchurches / organic churches readily and naturally spring up in everyday settings such as homes, workplaces, campuses and even in outdoor settings throughout the world. Indeed, this is an observable pattern that stretches from the pages of the New Testament to the present day again and again.

Empowering the Total Membership

Okay, so we know that the church is not a building. It is the body of believers throughout time and across the world. Once we grasp this, the next question becomes one of empowerment. What will it take to activate and equip believers to truly engage their mission as Christ-followers? Church leaders are called by Scripture to **"prepare God's people for works of service"** (Ephesians 4: 12). Therefore this becomes a key and "essential" question.

For some time now, organizational management experts have identified the so-called "Pareto Principle" at work in a wide variety of institutions – including the traditional church. It is otherwise known as the 80-20 rule. Simply stated, it asserts that 80 percent of the effects come from 20 percent of the causes. Sometimes known as the "law of the vital few", Mr. Vilfredo Pareto's principle is one with which many church leaders are well-acquainted. For example church leadership guru John Maxwell applies this "law' to church life when he observes:

"Time—20 percent of our time produces 80 percent of the results.

Counseling—20 percent of the people take up 80 percent of our time.

Reading—20 percent of a book contains 80 percent of the content.

Donations—20 percent of the people will give 80 percent of the money.

Speech—20 percent of our presentation produces 80 percent of the impact.

Picnic—20 percent of the people will eat 80 percent of the food." (1)

No disrespect to either Mr. Pareto or Mr. Maxwell but it must be pointed out that, where the Spirit of the Lord is concerned, some "laws" are made to be broken!

The simple fact is that in all my years in professional ministry I have never witnessed the level of total participation in the life and ministry of the Kingdom of God as much as I have in the past two years in our house church setting. This is not limited to a particular aspect of church life, either. From tiny tots to seniors, male and female, the total membership of our house church is hands on with the life, ministry and mission of our body of believers. In the words of Vineyard founding leader John Wimber, "everyone gets to play".

"But Bill", (you may be thinking), "your church is small enough to fit into a living room". Exactly. This means that everyone feels needed. This means that there is something everyone can contribute. This means there is time and space in our gatherings for everyone to have the opportunity to participate. It's so biblical it's scary!

"When you meet, one will sing, another will teach, another will tell some special revelation God has given, one will speak in an unknown language, while another will interpret what is said. But everything that is done must be useful to all and build them up in the Lord" (I Corinthians 14: 26, NLT). This, my friends, is as "real" as church gets!

From breakfast potluck to Bible study, *your* contribution is wanted and needed at our church. I have watched seven year old children lay their hands in prayer upon our teens and adults as they call upon the Lord for healing. I have benefitted from the insights of teens as they have commented on the Scriptures. I have stood in awe as they have served up meals for the homeless, written and performed their own Christmas plays, and held free car washes for our local crisis pregnancy clinic. Meanwhile, we adults bring sausages and fruit salads to the weekly breakfast meal, share a testimony or inspired prophetic word during our Sunday meetings, and operate the free face-painting booth at the neighborhood outreach festivals we have put together. From the packing of gifts for Filipino orphans to prayer-walking the neighborhood, no one feels unqualified, unwanted or unimportant.

While I know that God has many faithful, hardworking and wonderful servants in "Big Church" the logistics and culture of a typical weekend worship gathering is far more suited to the Pareto Principle than to the Apostle Paul Principle as cited above from I

Corinthians 14. Sadly, author Jim Rutz may have stated the truth all too well when he wrote:

> *"From 11 to 12 Sunday, you're just another pretty face in the crowd. Custom walls you off in your own space and silences your voice – except for song and responsive reading... The (Worship) service would be exactly the same without you. You know that. Your impact on it is like an extra gallon of water going over Niagra Falls."* (2)

To me, this doesn't mean that Big Church is "bad". There is a lot of good that goes on wherever and whenever God's people gather to lift up His Name, reach out to the lost and build up believers. It does mean, however, that a more intimate and interactive setting is necessary if believers are ever going to experience the full Body of Christ *in action* (and not just "in attendance"). This, of course, is what is envisioned for the Church in the New Testament.

A Missional Focus

Left to themselves, small groups often become ingrown and exclusive. Church researcher J.D. Payne recognizes this in his book *Missional House Churches* wherein he distinguished "missional" house churches from other types. "I use the term *missional*," he writes, "to distinguish house churches that engage the culture with the gospel, make disciples, and plant churches from those house churches that do not". For the purposes of his study, then, Payne looked for house churches that were planting out at least one new congregation every three years and that registered at least one new baptism each year (2).

As a national missionary with the North American Mission Board of the Southern Baptist Convention and a professor of Evangelism and Church Planting, J.D. Payne was surprised at his findings. As he put the focus of his studies on those thirty three different house churches that met his criteria of being "missional" he learned that:

- 80% had been meeting for less than ten years.
- Average house church membership was 14 to 17 individuals.
- The average number of baptisms in the previous year was from 4 to 6.
- The average number of new churches planted by existing congregations also averaged from 4 to 6. (2)

Payne further observed that "many of these leaders saw themselves functioning as primarily church planters, teachers, leadership developers, and mentors/coaches for local church pastors/elders. The leaders were overseeing and leading networks of churches, rather than a single congregation". (3) These figures are even more compelling when compared to the statistics coming from the majority of traditional churches – especially (Payne notes) those of a strong evangelical tradition such as the Southern Baptist churches of America. "Presently, over 80 percent of our churches are not experiencing substantial expansion growth", he writes. At least 31.3 percent of the 43,000 Southern Baptist churches in the U.S. registered no baptisms in 2003. Payne quotes Thom Rainer of Lifeway Christian Resources who declares that about 96% of American churches do NOT meet the criteria for being effective evangelistic churches (4).

The need to maintain a missional focus is clear – as is the evidence that microchurches are quite capable of consistently making disciples and planting new churches. My conviction is that the high level of relationship that develops between members of a typical house church makes it especially important that they remain strong in their outward mission. Otherwise, inertia will tend to cause them to become ingrown.

A Christ-Centered Ethos

Every community or society has an *ethos*. According to *Dictionary.com*, an ethos is: *"the fundamental character or spirit of a culture; the underlying sentiment that informs the beliefs, customs, or practices of a group or society; dominant assumptions of a people or period"* (6). Organic expressions of the church are distinguished by their Christ-focused, Christ-centered ethos. The "character or spirit" of that culture is Jesus. The "underlying sentiment that informs the beliefs, customs, or practices of that group" is how to glorify Jesus, grow in the knowledge of Jesus, share Jesus, live Jesus, and express Jesus. The "dominant assumption" is that it is not enough to be "family". It is not enough to feel "connected". It is not even enough to care for others outside the group. It is about a focus on the crucified and risen Son of God as leader, as center and as the ultimate justification for the existence of a house church.

In his book *The Forgotten Ways,* author Alan Hirsch further underscores the need to have Jesus Christ at the very center of the identity, the function, the "ethos" of the church:

> "I wish to briefly restate here what seems to be an obvious fact, but one that is often overlooked. For authentic missional Christianity, Jesus the Messiah plays an *absolutely* central role. Our identity as a movement, as well as our destiny as a people, is inextricably linked to Jesus – the Second Person of the Trinity."

The Apostle Paul underscores the centrality of Christ to the gathered community when he insists that the authentic presence of the Holy Spirit inspires the confession of Jesus as Lord: **"Therefore I tell you that no one who is speaking by the Spirit of God says, "Jesus be cursed," and no one can say, "Jesus is Lord," except by the Holy Spirit"** (I Corinthians 12:3).

There was a time in the history of the people of God when they lived a Temple-centered life. Sacrifices to the One God, Yahweh, were made there. The sacred feasts of the nation were held nearby that holy space. Priests, set apart by divine commission, attended to its sacred grounds, conducted its sacred functions and served the sacred purposes for which the Temple existed. Religious experts taught in its outer courts and, once each year, the people relied upon the special act of the High Priest to secure atonement for their sins in its most inward and sacred chamber. But the Scriptures declare that this is no longer the case for Jesus has rightfully claimed all the focus that was once commanded by the Holy Building of old. For evermore Jesus Christ *is* The Temple (John 2: 19; Rev. 21:22). He *is* the High Priest (Heb. 6:20). He *is* the sacrifice (I John 2:2). And He has gathered us unto Himself to bear witness to these things as His living temple, built without human hands. It is in the called out community of Christ, gathered in His Name, that the presence of God authentically dwells -- through Christ -- and by the Spirit (2 Cor. 6:16; I Peter 2:5).

The call of Christ's followers, then, is to exalt Him inasmuch as **"God placed all things under his feet and appointed him to be head over everything for the church"** (Eph. 1:22). Should anything or anyone else (even "good" things or "talented" people) supplant the believing community's focus on Christ as Lord of all and Head of the Body, the true destiny, purpose and power of that community will be thrown off balance and its true calling will either be diluted or, perhaps, completely missed altogether.

This is one of the beautiful things about the simplicity and potential focus of the microchurch – there is far less in the practical or spiritual environment to distract from the opportunity for every member to focus on Christ and exalt Him as the true center of that church's existence, mission and fellowship. The outworking of this fact extends throughout the life of the Body. It is not the charismatic "up-front" personality, the awe-inspiring religious edifice, the dazzling production values of the music, drama or multi-media communications that will receive the focus. It is, potentially, Christ and Christ alone who will occupy center stage – provided, of course, that the gathered community lives into its unique opportunity to put and keep Him there. The purity of this focus and the way it organizes everything else within the life of the gathered body of believers is certainly one of the things I have most enjoyed about simple church life.

Of all of the "essentials" this chapter has described, a Christ-centered ethos is the most essential of all.

In the next chapter, we will look at how a commitment to a simple and focused mission can shape the development of a homegrown community of faith.

(1) John Maxwell, …..

(2) James H. Rutz, *The Open Church,* The Seed Sowers, 1992, Introduction, p.1

(3) J.D. Payne, *Missional House Churches,* Paternoster Publishers, 2007, pps. 8, 9

(4) Ibid, pps. 50 and 59

(5) Ibid, p. 60

(6) http://dictionary.reference.com/browse/ethos

(7) Alan Hirsch, *The Forgotten Ways,* Brazos Press, 2006, p.94

One example is the percentage of people who practice their spiritual gifts to help their church grow. In churches with less than 100 in attendance, it's 31 percent. You can say that's not much. But if you compare that with churches of over 1,000 in attendance, which average only 17 percent, you see there is a decline in quality. In all areas except one, the quality decreases with the size of the church.

Chapter Five

A Mission to Everyday Places

"Go spend the day down at Johnny's Cafe
All kinds of people there with plenty to say…
Now if Jesus were here I think we'd find Him today,
Down at Johnny's Café"

John Fischer, *Johnny's Café,* 1978

* * * * * * *

"Empowering everyday people to take the ministry of Jesus to everyday places."

(Mission Statement of Vineyard at Home)

* * * * * * *

It was Saturday night, and the large living room was jammed with teenagers and young adults. Most of the crowd had brought a recently purchase Bible with them for the evening of Bible study, prayer and singing. I was one such person, age 15, ready to learn what it means to follow Jesus. I had just purchased my own Bible at the local J.C. Penny store. It had a zipper that ran around the edge and it featured the words of Jesus in red letters. Plus, it was written in the King's English with all the "thees" and "thous" you could ask for. I couldn't have been more impressed if it had been carved from solid gold.

Our Bible Study group teacher was barely twenty years old. His long hair flowed well past his shoulders and his spiral-bound notebook was packed with his freshest insights on the meaning of Scripture. As the evening progressed, he told us what the Bible said about God, about Jesus Christ and our need to be saved by faith. He talked about the last days. He talked about the Holy Spirit. He talked about being baptized in water and in the Spirit and about how important it was to seek God, to pray, to read the Bible and to share our faith with others. The roomful of young people hung on his words as if he were Moses fresh from a visit with God on Mount Sinai. And no one listened more closely or attentively than I.

On Sunday mornings, a smaller number of us often returned to the same private home that housed the big Saturday night Bible Study meeting. Once in awhile, a group of us would carpool from there to various local churches to attend a worship service together. Looking back, I think we enjoyed the shock value of walking into one of these traditional church settings with our long hair, our big Bibles and our t-shirts and flip-flops. Hey: we were Christians, too – as serious about our faith as anyone! We may not have *looked the part* but we definitely *had the heart*.

These Sunday hang-out times often included some kind of lunch meal. Eating together was an important way to connect and get to know one another. Around the table, we would talk about Jesus, our lives, popular music and how incredibly hot it was in our hometown of Phoenix, Arizona. Later in the afternoon, we might end up back at our "home base" – the house on 7th Street near Encanto Park – where we would read and discuss the Bible, pull out a guitar or two, or otherwise laze away a sweet Sunday afternoon. We might even head over to the nearby park to share our faith with some of the stoners that could reliably be found on "hippie hill" in front of the big outdoor bandshell.

On one particular Sunday afternoon in the Spring of 1971, the Bible Study leader with the long hair knelt down to pray with me on the living room floor of the home where we met for Bible Study and fellowship. Laying his hands upon me, he began to ask God to fill me with the power of the Holy Spirit. The surge of peace and grace that came over me as he prayed was unforgettable. Quietly, I found myself releasing this inflow of energy in an inspired prayer language we referred to as "the gift of tongues". We understood this to be an uninstructed language of prayer to God given in the moment by the Spirit. After awhile, I retreated to the back patio area where a beautiful Arizona sunset was already in progress. Waves of peace filled my soul and I felt as if I was seeing the splendor in the skies for the very first time. "If this is what Christianity is about", I thought to myself, "then I want nothing more than to know Jesus more and to follow Him for the rest of my life".

Something Old, Something New

These were my simple beginnings as a Christian - the primal motions of my newfound faith. No matter how sophisticated and "churchified" I would become over the years that followed, these early experiences of prayer, witness, fellowship and growth were the things that formed me as a Christ-follower. As I look back and compare my early Christian experience to the things I learned thereafter; it occurs to me that none of my foundations were laid within the program of a local church. There were no classes to take, no bases to round, no cards to fill out and sign. Simple was good. Organic was the order of the day. We dressed plainly. We met in a home. I was baptized in a river. We shared our faith in parks, on the streets and at school. We prayed together in the desert. This was how we rolled.

My purpose in recounting these things is not to make a good/bad comparison between formal church life and my own informal foundations as a believer. It is simply to point out that the environment of my early faith formation was geared towards reaching, teaching and releasing people in simple fashion. From the beginning, I was trained to be "self-feeding" as a Christ-follower. Those of our company who had committed their lives to Christ would never dream of showing up to one of our meetings without their Bible. New believers shared their testimony of salvation with others within days if not minutes of their conversion! There were no ordained "professionals" leading our ministry or solving our problems. Our elders were young men who were just a little farther ahead in their Christian walk than most of the rest of us. Their job was to study the Scriptures and then share what they were learning with us so we could all be built up in the faith. And they were motivated to keep at it if they wanted to stay ahead of the pack because all of us were hungry to learn, discuss and apply the Scriptures.

Let me be clear: this environment was far from perfect. There were gaps and holes in our operations and structure that a formal church congregation fills as a matter of course. Compared to the "pros" in the organized churches, we were playing sandlot ball – improvising as we went and learning the game from scratch. We had plenty of ups and downs. Outbreaks of jealousy, personal immaturities, flaws in character and doctrinal zig-zags were all part of the mix. There was, however, a key difference between my first faith community and the more traditionally organized church environments I joined and led over the years that followed. Primarily it was this: we understood ourselves to be *disciples* who were expected to own our maturity in Christ as opposed to *consumers* of church-based goods and services.

Later, after graduating Bible School, I set my sights on becoming a full-time professional pastor in a local church with an emphasis on youth ministry. By that time, I had become involved in a couple of different churches, both very large and rather small in size. I had learned some initial lessons of how traditional church was done, so to speak. I had been exposed to church polity and government as well as to the centrality of

Sunday morning worship services. It was clear that in the life of the traditional church, Sunday morning was treated as the key place and time for "ministry" to happen.

I learned about preaching three point sermons and how to hold an "altar call". I was exposed to the weekly printed bulletin and to organized Sunday School programs – complete with purchased curriculum and dedicated teachers. I learned about the midweek prayer meetings and other weekday church services and how youth groups were organized and developed. Looking back, I can see that it really does take some time and effort to get familiar with all the things that make up a local church and learn one's place within such a system.

As a newlywed and new Bible School grad in my twenties, I was finally offered my first opportunity to serve full time on the staff of a wonderful local church. I was very fortunate that my mentors and fellow church family members happened to be great people. They showed patience with my mistakes, enthusiasm for my ideas and love for Robin and me and our growing family.

Of course, the bread-and-butter of our church life was the Sunday morning worship service. We held two morning services and one evening gathering each Sunday. There were also youth group meetings, a few home fellowship groups, prayer meetings, staff meetings and other get-togethers for me to regularly attend. In addition, there were occasional denominational gatherings and other meetings and pow-wows where pastors and assistant church leaders could come together for denominational shop talk, fellowship and instruction. As a young adult, I had fully transitioned from a style of faith that was loosely structured, simply constituted and completely focused on a simple mission of following Jesus and leading others to do the same to a far more sophisticated Christian life. Who knew, for example, that church people and their leaders spent so much time in meetings and meetings about other meetings!

Fast Forward

Over the course of my adult life, my church and professional ministry experience continued to deepen. In the mid-1980's, Robin and I relocated in order to become a part of an exciting mega church back in Orange County, California. At that time, the Anaheim Vineyard was the flagship congregation of the most remarkable Christian movement I had ever encountered and we wanted to be a part of it. After a couple of years we left that church in order to help a very charismatic leader plant a new church in another part of our county. After this, I came to join the staff of a different Vineyard church that grew to attract about a thousand people to its weekly worship services. This church also featured a thriving ministry to the poor, an active Christian elementary school and other impressive programs and outreaches. After a wonderful decade of service to that church, Robin and I were given the blessing of our leaders to go out from that place and plant a new Vineyard church of our own.

These various congregations differed significantly in size, leadership style, history and emphasis. Nevertheless, they shared a common philosophy of ministry. It was an approach that focused on the creation of attractive, spiritually dynamic, practically helpful or culturally relevant programs and outreaches. It was hoped that these things would increase the number of those who come regularly to our home base campus and, eventually, join themselves to our church family as an involved member. A ministry "win" was when someone began showing up on Sundays and then began to express their interest in becoming a baptized believer, a faithful giver, an active small group member or a committed volunteer in one of our church programs. You might say that INVOLVEMENT was the unspoken benchmark of Christian growth and spiritual maturity. It was assumed that the people who volunteered their time, talent and treasure to the life and ministries of the church developing as a follower of Jesus.

This meant that, over the course of my life as a full-time ministry professional and church planter, I spent countless hours trying to answer the question: *"how do we get people to come through the door of this church so that we can share our lives and our message with them?"* This led me to be involved in many, many outreaches over the years. Among them were various concerts, conferences, worship services, special events, classes, groups, renewal meetings, prayer meetings, healing services, holiday events, care ministries and counseling sessions that were aimed at drawing people to us so we could reach them for Christ. And, without a doubt, there were people who were "reached" in these ways. However, without our realizing it, we were training ourselves and others to think that *real ministry* took place within the walls of the church where the professionals could skillfully reach into the lives of visitors.

This is no joke. Much of the evangelical church has adopted and perpetuated an *attractional* notion of ministry. Each year, a number of prominent conferences, coaching programs, books, training materials and other support systems are offered to leaders and pastors. The promise is that, by adopting methods and outreaches that can successfully attract and retain satisfied people to their congregation, it can grow in size, in influence and in mission. This left the job of taking ministry to everyday people and environments to so-called "parachurch" organizations such as Campus Crusade for Christ, The Fellowship of Christian Athletes, Prison Fellowship, new church planters, missionaries, and many others. Is this really what Jesus had in mind when He commissioned His disciples to "go into all the world"? I don't think so.

The sad thing about our stubborn commitment to attract what we might call church consumers is that it tends to waste a large amount of resources and manpower on fine-tuning our brand so that our church can compete well in the religious marketplace (I realize this language is cynical, but – believe me – as an insider

I know that it is not inaccurate). As a result, few churches have done little to actually penetrate and change the culture around them. A visiting Chinese house church leader who was on his first trip to the West put it well when he noted: "You (Western church leaders) do so little with so much, while we do so much with so little." These words may be painful, but can we really deny that they are true? Ouch.

Another Way

In my experience, a return to a "homegrown" ministry approach provides us with a healthy alternative to the predominant *attractional* philosophy to ministry that has become some deeply rooted in Western evangelicalism. In visualizing Vineyard at Home, we hoped to accomplish a central mission of "empowering everyday people to take the ministry of Jesus to everyday places". I am happy to report that this is an approach we have been able to adopt, verify, maintain and enjoy. It is a mission that puts us back in touch with the essential beauty and simple truth of the Gospel. It has increased our joy, deepened our personal commitment to maturity and developed a community that has much in common with what we see in the New Testament book of Acts and the epistles.

Clearly, the most common environment for the ministry of the Gospel of the Kingdom of God we see in the Bible is not the Temple in Jerusalem or a local synagogue. It is the "everyday places" where our Lord and His apostles and evangelists enrolled men and women of many kinds into taking a part in the ongoing ministry of Jesus. In the New Testament, the ministry of the Word and the Spirit takes place in homes, in open fields, on the shoreline, and many other locations where people lived their real, daily lives. How is it, then, that so many of us who believe in our times have become so focused on *containing* the ministry of Jesus within the walls of the buildings we have erected "for His glory"? How did we get so focused on programs and institutions? How did we come to put so much faith in our ministry professionals to do the work of the ministry?

How is it that we came to so readily pour our energies into getting people on our turf where we could influence them to follow Christ in a "churchified" setting? Can't we see how this actually sets people up to struggle with how to effectively and naturally translate their faith into everyday settings and relationships? When Vineyard founder John Wimber proposed that "the 'meat' is in the street", I understood him to be pointing us outward to the community settings of home, school, neighborhood and workplace. Nevertheless, if you follow the resource allotments in most of our church settings, it will lead us to the inescapable conclusion that we actually believe the 'meat' is in the church sanctuary, youth room, or fellowship hall!

Bubble Up

Now, let's be clear: you will hardly find a church that doesn't state somewhere on paper that they are all about "equipping the saints" and "mobilizing believers for ministry to the community". However, many of these same churches turn around and train their people that their key role is to get their friends and family to come to a church service or event where someone else (usually a ministry professional) will actually reach them for Christ. It doesn't take long for everyday believers to get the *real* message: "Hey kids - don't try this at home". First they must undergo "evangelism training" so they can learn to share Christ "out there". But it is actually quite natural to share our faith in everyday relationships if we are not overly surrounded by the so-called "church bubble".

The fight to escape the church bubble is a phenomenon familiar to anyone who has been a churched believer for any significant length of time. That is because church programs often require the bulk of our resources as measured in both money and man hours. I have noticed that pastors and ministry coordinators eye mature newcomers with the same kind of interest a lion shows in his or her potential lunch-on-the-hoof! After a few visits, seasoned believers are quickly sought out for recruitment by the children's ministry, the men's fellowship, the worship team, the outreach committee or a hundred other departments or ministries of the church. Once they have been enrolled, they may easily wind up "at the church" three or four times per week. It's easy to see why these folks lose touch with the everyday people in their lives – the people with whom they might otherwise share their faith in far more natural ways.

The Gospel Blimp Lives On

I remember reading an insightful little fable some years ago called: *The Gospel Blimp*. It is the story of George and Ethel and their friends and fellow church members in Middletown, USA. These believers are appropriately concerned about the spiritual condition of their next door neighbors and believe the time has come to take action to reach them. But it is when a blimp flies over this gathering of church members one day that things begin to get interesting. Before long, the would-be evangelists become captivated by the possibilities of using a blimp to reach people for Christ. Thanks to some serious efforts; a used blimp is purchased, a pilot hired and the flying machine is comprehensively equipped to proclaim God's message.

Eventually, this "Gospel Blimp" tows banners with biblical messages, "firebombs" local residents with dropped leaflets, and loudly broadcasts Christian music and programming over its powerful speaker system. How can such proclamation not be a good thing? Trouble ensues, however, as some of the members of the blimp team begin to harbor serious doubts about their strategy, their methods and the ever-increasing sacrifices that "Gospel Blimps, Incorporated" and it's Commander (a fellow named Herm) are making upon them. And, by the way, whatever happened to the unreached next door neighbors that inspired all this in the first place?

It seems to me that, without knowing it, many churches have become "stationary Gospel Blimps" parked at the corner of Church Street and Main. They post clever messages on their signs, loudly broadcast God's message within their four walls, and educate believers on the importance of "reaching the world for Christ" (by getting them to fill the empty seats at church with their friends and family). And why not? Conventional churches programs and properties are expensive to maintain, to keep well-staffed and to expand. Their leaders have a vested interest in drawing larger and larger crowds to official events and programs – if only from a financial point-of-view. The hoped for increase in attendance will validate the assumption that the church is spiritually prosperous. And, I can tell you from experience that no pastor likes to admit that their numbers are low while talking shop with fellow church leaders!

Insincere?

This is not to say that all – or even most -- churches are insincere about fulfilling their mission. In my experience, most church leaders truly care about reaching their community for Christ. And, of course, there are wonderful churches that do much ministry off campus and who strongly support everyday place ministry through by empowering their members to be innovative and to meet real needs "out there". There is, however, a mindset that exists in church circles that provides church members with plenty of reasons to neglect the kinds of relationships, service points, and personal involvements which would most naturally allow the reality of God's kingdom to break in to this world's everyday places. Like George and Ethel, too many churches are so invested in Gospel Blimps that they don't have time to think creatively, imaginatively and simply about how they might share Christ in real life, real time relationships and environments.

Teapot Evangelism

I know of a lady who "gets it" about the difference between blimp evangelism and simple and focused ministry in everyday places. She begins by purchasing inexpensive teapots at garage sales and keeping a few on hand. Then when she hears of a neighbor or friend who is sick, struggling or in need of a lift, this "teapot evangelist" goes to work. First, she plants a colorful plant or flower in one of her teapots. Then she takes her attractive little gift to the door of the person she has in mind and presents it to them with a smile, some care and, perhaps, a prayer. I'd be willing to bet this woman never graduated from one of those evangelism training classes offered at the church. I have rarely seen such trainings inspire something as simple, warm, relational and natural as her teapot ministry.

Keeping things simple, focused, real and accessible is the kind of ministry Jesus and the Apostles modeled in the New Testament. It's the kind of ministry we see in the actions of the Teapot Lady, the in-dorm Bible study group, and a thousand and one other imaginative and incarnational expressions of "ministry in everyday places". No matter who we are, let's break the bubble and show up where it counts for Christ and His kingdom "out there"!

Chapter Six

Leadership

Church leadership is the subject of countless
books, conferences, seminary classes, board meetings,
dissertations and controversies. And just because this
mega-conversation has been going on around the world
and across the centuries does not mean it is going to end
anytime soon! Indeed, digesting church leadership
paradigms and applying them has occupied many, many
hours of my own life as a Bible School student, leader,
local church pastor and active participant in church life.
It has been rather sobering, then, for me to realize how
little of the church leadership training I have received
over the years applies to the kind of homegrown church
ministry that now fills my life.

This is not without reason. It is my observation
that a good deal of the conversation about contemporary
church leadership blends the latest corporate and social
leadership axioms together with selected biblical
passages. The attempt is then made to apply these
principles to the life and mission of the local church. If
it is not openly promised, success (as measured by such
indicators as higher attendance, increased
"effectiveness" and bigger budgets) is presumed to be
within the reach of pastors who will simply put these
principles to work in their congregational environment.

Honestly, I think it does take a special leadership
blend to effectively and efficiently operate a large church

organization and, when this is done well, it is admirable. The key leaders must have a knack for understanding systems, managing resources, motivating large numbers of people and establishing a viable corporate culture in a sizeable setting. The members of large churches look to their leaders for both organizational efficiency and spiritual vitality – a rare blend, indeed! And, because leadership insights continue to be developed and redefined, it is necessary for the leaders of larger churches to stay abreast of the latest wave of ever-evolving principles of organizational leadership. Studies show that it is against all odds for classically trained local church leaders to successfully achieve this spiritual/corporate blend, successfully sustain their role in it, and remain at the helm over long periods of time without succumbing to burnout, moral failure or other hazards of large-scale professional ministry.

In contrast to this, I note a very different leadership spirit in the organic church environment. Indeed, many of the organizational principles and practices deemed necessary in the traditional church context – especially in cases where congregations are large and finely-tuned – have little to no meaning in the organic church environment. In fact, many of these truisms must be set aside or even vigorously *un*learned in the microchurch modality.

This is not a mere matter of comparative size or numbers. It is more about the fact that the fundamental building blocks of Christian life and mission are assimilated and developed very differently in an organic environment. Resource allotment, problem solving, decision making, spiritual maturity, personal empowerment and a host of other issues show up differently in the simplified and deconstructed life of the homegrown church. At Vineyard at Home, we have struggled with the fact that so many of the "rules" of church life have changed. This shift is both confusing (at times) and extremely liberating!

This is not to say that "church leadership" does not exist in the simple church. It absolutely does. Nor am I implying that quality leadership doesn't matter to the homegrown church for that would also be a foolish thing to affirm. Every area of life is affected by the presence of understanding and qualified leadership. Every system that seeks to fulfill its reason for being requires it. Organic churches are no exception. They exist to engage the same timeless missions of the Great Commission and Great Commandment that all authentically missional churches must grapple with. Furthermore, they also share in the ongoing call for gathered believers to glorify God, build up one another, and extend God's merciful and life-giving grace in spiritual and practical ways. As with any group that lives into a call that will ultimately benefit others; microchurches must become organized, empowered, sustainable, accountable and able to be corrected. But that is not to say that they must become institutional. In fact, they had better not fall into that trap!

Death by Institutionalism

We are living in a day when a growing disdain for institutionalism can be found throughout society. This anti-institutional sentiment can be found in the business world, in education, in the arts, and in the church world, too. The kind of religious institutionalism that disengages believers from their world and encapsulates them in a church bubble is well documented. Clearly, this is not the assignment God gave His Son in His incarnation. Nor is it the assignment Jesus gave to His Church as His kingdom ambassadors. And yet, the propensity of religious organizations to get lost in an institutional hall of mirrors leads to a sad loss of passion and vitality. It also results in a dimming of spiritual vision and – in some cases – an eventual rejection of faith itself!

In his book *Organic Leadership*, author Neil Cole makes some startling observations about the distorting effects of institutionalism on church leadership when he writes:

> "Inside the institution (the leaders) are important people, educated people. Outside they are nothing, with no clout, no power, nothing impressive. It is dangerous when the institution becomes the leader's source of identity and purpose. Soon the leader feels compelled to give his or her life to maintaining the institution. In essence the leader is a prisoner and cannot imagine life on the outside" (1).

This is death by institutionalism. In this upside-down world, the higher one climbs the institutional ladder the more he or she is in danger of becoming a candidate for disillusionment. This leads to case after case of burnout, isolation, indifference, immorality and other personal and spiritual maladies. It is ironic to see institutional advancement sometimes become the very thing that increases one's distance from God, His passion, His mission and His family. So what is the homegrown alternative? What does healthy leadership look like in an organic church?

Eldership

In an organic modality, leaders are truly "elders" – the older brothers and sisters or spiritual "fathers" and "mothers" of the community. Their esteem and influence is not so much rooted in institutional credentials and positions as it is in their spiritual maturity and overall way of life. They do not take on the persona of a corporate manager or CEO. Their eldership arises out of relationships they make within the community of faith and the respect they earn by both following the Lord and inspiring others to follow Him, too.

As in the more traditional churches, teaching is an important gift in the life of an organic church elder. However, it may not be best expressed in the lecturing fashion with which we have become familiar in classic sermon delivery. The microchurch allows for teachers to interact with disciples in real time in a more Socratic give-and-take. Teaching and training includes both thoughtful presentation, discussion and an intentional focus on application. The wise elder knows that posing the right questions is as important as supplying the right answers. In short, elders teach with their lives. This is the biblical notion of elder/teachers.

A thorough reading of the New Testament epistles emphasizes this notion of eldership again and again. It also explains why incongruity between what teachers/elders say and how they live is simply not tolerable in the milieu of the New Testament church. As John Wimber used to quip, above all else: "Elders *eld*". And it is through their "elding" that they provide leadership to the community of faith. Therefore the qualifications for eldership in the organic church community are different than the qualifications usually cited as requirements for a corporate management position. Simply put, the qualifications for eldership begin with *a life well lived.* Note, for example, the qualifications outlined by Paul in I Timothy, chapter three:

> *"Now the overseer must be above reproach, the husband of but one wife, temperate, self-controlled, respectable, hospitable, able to teach, not given to drunkenness, not violent but gentle, not quarrelsome, not a lover of money. He must manage his own family well and see that his children obey him with proper respect. (If anyone does not know how to manage his own family, how can he take care of God's church?)*

He must not be a recent convert, or he may become conceited and fall under the same judgment as the devil. He must also have a good reputation with outsiders, so that he will not fall into disgrace and into the devil's trap" (I Timothy 3: 2-7, NIV).

Among other things, this list of what Paul looked for in a church "overseer" (NIV, ESV, NASB, etc) or "bishop" (KJV, RSV, ASV, etc) focuses on the qualities of good character, emotional balance, a healthy commitment to one's own family, financial sobriety and a generally respectable way of life that reflects the priorities of a Christ-follower. The inference is that the overseer must live a life worthy of emulation; i.e. "how many more like *you* do you want?" According to Paul, the way an elder lives is the key component to how they lead, teach and influence others. Their personal character is worthy of emulation and the spiritual DNA they manifest shows forth its quality in both teaching and life-on-life contact.

This *does not* mean elders are perfect people. It *does* mean that they are people who "walk in the light as He is in the light" and, by so doing, promote an atmosphere of "fellowship with one another" described by the Apostle John in I John 1: 7. Elders do not hide their faults in the shadows. They do not put on airs or pretend to be something they are not. Instead, they model how one comes to Christ as a person who wishes to continue "growing in grace and in the knowledge of our Lord Jesus Christ" (2 Peter 3: 18). They must be "able to teach" (I Timothy 3: 2), of course. But such teaching is not limited to the transference of truth by means of formal communications. What is "caught" is as important as what is "taught" in a homegrown environment.

In light of this, note the way Paul applies the standards of a teacher to himself when addressing his young protégé Timothy: *"You, however, know all about my teaching, my way of life, my purpose, faith, patience, love, endurance..." (2 Timothy 3: 10)*. For Paul, teaching and doing the things that attend "sound doctrine" make up whole piece of cloth (see, for example, I Timothy 1: 9, 10).

Family Trust

The relational environment of the microchurch/organic church amplifies this aspect of discipleship. In a larger traditional church context, it is possible to go for years without having any significant personal interaction with top echelon leaders. Not so with the organic church environment. In that context, leadership involves a good deal of interpersonal relationship between the leaders (elders) and members of a given Body. It is much more of a family than an institution and, as such, features all the benefits and challenges of family life. While the relational risks are higher in such a tight knit environment the rewards are also potentially far greater.

On a practical level, this interconnectivity leads to a collegiate environment in the microchurch modality. Once the group builds trust and matures sufficiently, a good many of the key decisions regarding their life together, questions of financial management, expressions of mission, church discipline, and other related matters can be processed by the entire church family and not just by a select few. Ideally, a mature homegrown body of believers can come together to seek out what "seems good to the Holy Spirit and to us" (Acts 15: 28) and then take action in light of their conclusions.

Maturity and Empowerment

For these reasons, a key task of an organic (versus an institutional) leader is to promote maturity within the family, church, business entity or other community they lead. This notion of maturity is defined as the ability of the system to actualize its full potential, function at its highest level and authentically maintain a commitment to the core purposes and reason for being. In a general sense, a mature entity is simply one that has been properly empowered to "come into its own". When applied to organic church life, a given body of believers displays maturity when it authentically proclaims the gospel of the kingdom in both word *and* works.

Effective leaders play an important part in this vision for maturity by helping members identify and utilize their spiritual gifts at an age appropriate level. Any church that successfully accomplishes this will be characterized by a spirit of inspiration, empowerment and risk-taking. This adventurous spirit will manifest itself in a wide variety of identifiable activities that involve all members in various ways, no matter what their age or sex. Just as we see in the Gospels (in the ministry of Jesus) and in the Book of Acts (in the lives of the Apostles and early community of believers), there is a consistent baseline mission that supports an endlessly variable stream of ministry encounters and opportunities. By contrast, institutionalism is characterized by its tendency towards predictability, stagnation and a sickening sense that the "same-old-same-old" is the name of the game.

Empowerment is evidenced in the way ideas, activities, spiritual vitality and inspiration is able to come from any number of sources within the group, not just the "top dogs". It is plain to everyone that not all members have the same gifts; nor do they all participate in the same ways. This is made abundantly clear by Paul in I Corinthians 12. However, there is nothing in the organic environment to suggest a clergy-laity split. Members are never to be treated as mere worker bees waiting for the senior pastor's vision statement to be unveiled before going active. In the microchurch environment the Spirit is able to speak to the group as a whole through any member. The entire Body is then responsible to weigh what the Spirit is saying and fashion an inspired response. This is something we have experienced again and again in our life together as Vineyard at Home. I find it to be exceptionally satisfying and fulfilling as a someone who values both community and outreach.

The Doing *is* The Training

In His way of living with and training His own disciples, Jesus modeled the reality that maturity can only be fully experienced *in the doing.* This is not to cast aside the legitimate development of intellectual and spiritual insights. But if we take the Lord's method of maturity as our model, we cannot miss the way He employed an approach to learning that can only come from life-on-life interpersonal connection: *"He appointed twelve–designating them apostles–**that they might be with Him** and that He might send them out to preach"* (Mark 3: 14, NIV – emphasis mine).

This notion of leadership and maturity is echoed by Paul in the first chapter of Romans. In this passage, he clearly anticipates a mutually beneficial relationship with the believers he addresses even though he is speaking to them in his authority as an apostle: *"I long to see you so that I may impart to you some spiritual gift to make you strong - that is, that you and I may be mutually encouraged by each other's faith" (Romans 1: 11, 12).* This kind of Christian maturity, and the style of leadership that will produce it, comes down to a matter of *doing things* together. The resulting exchange of spiritual gifts, opportunities for personal instruction and interpersonal debriefing will result in a "show and tell" approach to ministry training. In this way life together becomes a living School of the Spirit for all ages and maturity levels.

Bringing all this down to a practical level has been the most challenging and most fun part of our journey together. Ever since our initial formation we have been deconstructing the more traditional notion of the Senior Pastor as CEO in favor of an overseeing eldership that lives up close and personal with the family of believers. Nevertheless, I find that there are a few holdover roles and functions that have continued from my previous life as a local church pastor. For example, I still love to conduct weddings and officiate at memorial services or funerals. Additionally, we have retained our tax exempt status as a local church body. As a result, we maintain a formal Board for our non-profit religious corporation. I serve as the President of that Board. Most of the time; these things are largely invisible to the way we function together. I like to think of it as the way the lead goose leads the "V" formation in a flock of flying geese. As things change, that bird can either lead or fall back into the formation depending on what is warranted by a given situation.

At Vineyard at Home, many of our spending choices, mission decisions and problem-solving efforts are processed as a group and – so far – this works well. I also facilitate the Bible teaching portion of our worship gatherings on Sundays. However, it is done in the style of a discussion leader's role rather than that of a "sermonizer". I see this as a shepherd's role in that it allows me to better understand where the flock is in their ability to think through and apply biblical truth. After all, it is the scriptural role of a shepherd to "guard the flock" through teaching, example and forbearance. This suggests a sense of personal acquaintance with the members of the flock after the manner of Jesus, the ultimate Good Shepherd (see John 10: 11-15). "Hirelings" who seek to use the flock as a way to platform their own egos need not apply.

Summary

Church leadership in a simple church/organic church/microchurch/house church context will look different than it does in the traditional congregation. But – especially for those of us who are transitioning from a conventional church modality to an organic modality – the shift is a process that unfolds as the Body of believers adapts and reconfigures itself. I am okay with that process. In fact, I (usually) really enjoy it. I like what I see happening in the people who have engaged it with me and I like what I see happening in me. I wonder what your adventure in leadership will look like as you and your fellow Christ-followers find your way forward into a more organic form of church life and mission?

1. Neil Cole, *Organic Leadership,* Baker Books, Grand Rapids, 2009, p.34

Chapter Seven

Looking Ahead

"The more ministry we can do OFF the church campus, the better."

This is one of the assumptions I recently put before a gathering of pastors, traditional church members and ministry leaders, and house church folk for discussion*. Though it is a notion that may at first challenge the sensibilities of the highly churched; it ultimately has the power to stir energy, vision and creativity that can change the world. The future of Vineyard at Home and, indeed, the Church at large, is bound up in a sincere engagement of this notion.

Our Master, Jesus, and His Apostles brought the reality of God's rule to bear on the everyday places and everyday relationships of their day. Their most responsive audiences and most avid learners were fishermen (Peter and John), tax collectors (Matthew), businesswomen (Lydia), a revolutionary or two (Simon, the Zealot) and the like. It was their goal, during the days of their ministry, to reach *exactly* this kind of (everyday) person and it continues to be the agenda of Jesus as He ministers through us who follow Him in the present day.

The visible in-breaking of God's rule into human events, human relationships and human experience is the heart of the Gospel. This is evident in the words of what might be termed The Mission Statement of Jesus: **"The Spirit of the Lord is upon Me, because He has anointed Me to preach good news to the poor. He has sent me to proclaim freedom for the prisoners and recovery of sight for the blind, to release the oppressed, to proclaim the year of the Lord's favor"** (Luke 4:18, 19 – quoting Isaiah 61:1, 2). While it is undeniably wonderful when these telltale signs of the ministry of Jesus take place within the walls of a dedicated worship center it is even more wonderful when they take place in the context of neighborhoods, campuses, workplaces and other everyday environments. Why? Because the latter looks a lot more like what we read about ("the stuff", in the words of John Wimber) in the Bible.

Over the years I have noticed that when people get deeply "churchified" – meaning they locate nearly all of their religious identity and practice in church campus-based programs, ministries and worship services – they experience a sort of spiritual sickliness. In some cases, the more "committed" to church-centered activities they become, the more they seem to lack a truly healthy, vitalized spirituality. They often develop an increasing "us" (the churched) versus "them" (the unchurched) worldview which makes it hard for them to re-contextualize their faith in everyday environments – ones that lack the trappings of church culture.

Those immersed in church, church and more church necessarily spend less time volunteering in the community, socializing with the unchurched, and otherwise interacting with the very people their witness is most intended to impact. Even spouses, children, and other family members may wind up feeling jealous of the devotion to church activities exemplified by the deeply churched. The idea that greater church involvement serves as a reliable mark of Christian maturity is highly questionable and can lead to unnecessary personal and interpersonal conflicts. (1)

By contrast, however, we can see that some house churches become little more than Holy Huddles. These ingrown groups have a different kind of insulating, isolating effect on their members. While it is a potentially worthy thing to "go simple" and meet in homes and other everyday environments; it is only healthy if those environments are treated as staging areas for real life ministry and not just a different kind of religious destination point where people go to hide. Frankly, I'm put off by people who proclaim the correctness of their church models – so superior to the "Constantinian" church systems they reject – but who (ironically) do almost nothing to intentionally care for unreached peoples around them. Jesus didn't call us to go to every nation and fine-tune the perfect church. Nor did He command us to erect grand religious edifices in His Name. He sent us, as His followers, to proclaim the Good News of God's Kingdom and to demonstrate His saving, transforming power in the places and throught the relationships in which people transact their real lives.

This is only the story of the New Testament but it is also the story God wants to continue to tell through us in our time.

Imagining the Future

A mission to *empower everyday people to take the ministry of Jesus to everyday places* is one we believe to be sound, sustainable, flexible and biblically faithful. It has formed our Homegrown philosophy of ministry and a good deal of our structure and practice to this point. Therefore, our future will be defined - at least in part - by the ongoing quest to follow wherever this mission takes us. In addition, we intend to help other believers to hear this call and express it in their own contexts and environments as part of a diversified Network. In other words, it is not our dream to grow as *big* as possible (in the "megachurch" sense) but as *wide* as possible. That's because my experience has taught me that any church that truly engages The Great Commission and The Great Commandment is *bigger on the inside* than it is *on the outside*.

Presently, we imagine our future as pioneers who live on the edge rather than as ecclesiastical scientists who do little more than attempt to boil the church down to its component parts. What we have learned (and unlearned) so far serves as a baseline from which we will continue to improvise and explore as God leads us in the adventure of living as an expression of His called out community. If we maintain the will to refuse to settle for convention we can imagine invigorating opportunities for personal growth as well as outreach to others in our future. But we are not naïve idealists. We know there will always be problems to solve, corrections to make, and challenging relationships to manage. Isn't this the record of the New Testament as well as the history of the church throughout the ages?

It is not, therefore, our quest to build the "perfect church" and then freeze dry it for distribution. Instead, we are out to follow Jesus as best as we can in ways that are simple, reproducible, spiritually authentic, and humanly engaging. An example of what this looks like in real time recently came our way in the wake of a devastating Southern California deluge.

And the Mud Came a'tumblin' Down

A popular song from the 1970's asserts that "*it never rains in California but, girl, don't they warn 'ya? It pours, man it pours!*" That was certainly the case in the winter of 2010 when a fierce series of rain storms struck our region of California around Christmastime. This wintertime torrent was responsible for wreaking havoc in a number of area neighborhoods. It was especially destructive to those areas where recent wildfires had raised the potential for flooding and mudslides.

One such area, as it turned out, was the very neighborhood in which our Foothill Ranch House Church meets. It was there that, one morning about 3 a.m.; the heavy, liquefied soil from some of the hills behind about a dozen local homes gave way. This mudslide slammed into the backs of these homes before oozing around them into the street area in front. The results were overwhelming. In one case, an eight foot deep swimming pool completely filled with mud while the heavy slop was also stacked another three feet or so deep throughout the back and side yards. The inside of a number of homes were impacted also. The result was an unbelievable mess that would require thousands of dollars and many man hours to clean up and properly remove.

On the Sunday that followed; our House Church members discussed what could be done to help these neighbors. It was a little comical for our small group of children and adults to think that we could have any real impact on such a mess but we couldn't imagine doing nothing. So, we began by showing solidarity and concern in an instantly attainable way – we purchased restaurant gift cards to distribute to the residents of the damaged homes as a way of saying "we see what you're going through and we care".

Once the gift cards were purchased, we enclosed them in handmade greeting cards. Over the next several days our House Church hostess and some of her children went door-to-door to present our token of concern and care to the various homeowners. The feedback from the residents was very positive. Most were taken aback by the simple act of kindness expressed in these gifts. Some asked her about our church (was there really a "church" in their neighborhood despite the absence of any church building?). Some of these conversations were fairly brief while others were of a far more in-depth nature.

One such conversation sprang up between our house church hostess and the couple who owned the home with the mud-filled swimming pool. The result was the homeowners' invitation for our little church group to come by and inspect the storm damage for ourselves on the following Sunday. It was hoped we might be able to imagine some ways in which we could more specifically assist this family once we saw things up close for ourselves. After taking a tour through the overwhelming mud and slop we courageously declared to this family that "we are going to help you". Exactly how, we couldn't say at first but then our man Eric stepped up with a plan.

Sermon in the Mud

Eric is an adult member of our Foothill Ranch House Church who, among other things, leads our teenagers. Eric's "day job" is in construction-related. Out of all of us, he was the one who could truly assess the damage and take an educated guess at what it would take to clean it all up. Once he sized up the task, Eric got on the phone and began calling in favors from people he knew. These were people who had access to heavy equipment! Before long, a Bobcat, a backhoe and some dump trucks were mobilized and by the following weekend, our Homegrown cleanup project was underway!

Although most of us could only supply manual labor, I was stunned to see how willingly everyone worked. In addition to our House Church crowd, a swarm of other people showed up to help. Some were from our greater Vineyard at Home network. There were also neighbors, family members, and other helpers on site to help. The work progressed with amazing speed. Even representatives of the local homeowners association came to see for themselves what people were doing in the mud zone. It was, as the young people say, "epic"!

That weekend's Sunday Worship Gathering took place in the progressively "de-mudded" backyard of the swimming pool house. For a few moments the work stopped. The heavy equipment was switched off. The shovels were laid down. It was time to seize the moment and recognize what God had done - to celebrate, to pray, and to give thanks!

After giving time for people to share openly and spontaneously, I delivered a brief "sermon-in-the-mud":

> "The Bible does not declare that 'all things are good'", I reminded our ad hoc work force. "However, it does boldly state that 'all things *work together for good* for all those who love the Lord and are the called according to His purpose" (Romans 8:28). "It is not good that this horrible mudslide took place - but just look at how God has turned it for good in so many ways and in so many lives!"

Everyone agreed that we had seen God make something truly wonderful out of what began as a terrible disaster. After some more thanks and praise, we closed in a final word of prayer together. Then it was back to work!

By midday the bulk of the task was completed. The house church folks decided to throw together a BBQ to celebrate this milestone! As delicious food was prepared and shared with the neighbors and other work team members, we marveled again at how much had been accomplished in so little time. It may not have been on par with the biblical parting of the Red Sea but there was no doubt that a tremendous amount of mud was "parted" from two of the worst-hit homes in just one weekend. As I reflected back on the day it occurred to me that there was no cathedral or worship center on earth I would have rather worshipped in that morning. God was "in" that muddy scene just as surely and profoundly as He might be perceived to be "in" the grandest and most golden shrine!

It was about a week later when the owner of the worst hit house (the swimming pool place) showed up at the door of our house church host family's home. She had come to present a CD of an original song she had composed and recorded. She explained that the song was inspired by her family's experiences with the God-sent assistance they had received after on the heels of their biggest challenge. Although she does not identify herself with any particular faith community or religious persuasion, the title of her song, *Praise the Risen Lord,* says it all. The following Sunday, we listened to the song together during our house church worship gathering and marveled at the message the song's writer had received from our involvement – and where that message had pointed her heart: to the Risen Lord!

These are the kinds of experiences we anticipate for ourselves in the future. Our life as a Homegrown church encourages flexibility, simplicity, love and worship. It energizes a vision to not only learn the Bible and discuss its meaning but to truly apply it in ways that support our stated mission.

Multiplication

Our vision for the future involves a desire to share what we have learned with others in the hopes that the Homegrown approach will find new expression in an ever-widening Network. Ideally, younger generations would be drawn to the transferable elements of our model and to the willingness of our elders to mentor others in life-on-life relationships. This is, of course, something we see demonstrated in the New Testament in the relationship Paul had with Timothy and in other biblical texts as well. In a more contemporary context, I appreciate the way one respected African-American church leader expressed his convictions in these regards:

> *"I believe there are thousands of emerging apostles that have gifts within them and they are not being released because we don't have fathers that understand the apostolic calling*

and the [need to] release them like we should.
I believe we do have many young ministers with
apostolic callings who struggle to develop on
their own because there is no one in their
region that they are connected to that has a
heart to train and disciple them into their
gifting."

(John Eckhart, founder of Crusader Ministries,
Chicago, Illinois)

I believe that Mr. Eckhart is correct in identifying
an untapped opportunity to not only offer young people
formalized ministry training but personalized mentoring
through relationships with caring, wise and empowering
elders. During my younger years as a participant in the
Jesus People movement in America, I witnessed
examples of the positive differences good mentoring
makes as well as the disasters that result when even
those with significant spiritual gifts are forced to attempt
to develop as leaders without it.

The beauty of a Homegrown approach is the way
it lowers the bar for leadership training, spreads
participation and responsibility across the entire
assembly of Believers in a given situation, and retains a
focus on a passionate commitment to the mission at
hand. It goes without saying that simple structures are
more transferable than complicated ones. Less
institutional structures are more flexible. Relational
leadership training is more penetrating, formational and

sustainable (thanks to the vast range of today's communication options).

In our case, we believe we have now learned enough of the A, B, Cs of Homegrown church life and mission to offer assistance to those who would like to launch their own Homegrown churches. We will soon offer conferences, written materials, webinars and the like to make what we have learned available. In this way we hope to develop mentoring and coaching relationships with potential house church/microchurch leaders. We also want to continue to learn from others as we forge new relationships with other explorers and pioneers. Ultimately, our hope is that our Network will grow wider from both internal launches as well as through the mentoring of startup efforts begun by others.

* The recording is available from me on a CD at no charge. Email me at Bill@vcmn.org to get your copy. Make sure and include your email, name, address, and zip code.

(1) The famous Willow Creek Church association is currently engaged in a sobering review of these notions of maturity and ministry. For a helpful introduction to this, see the very well-presented video available at:

http://www.youtube.com/watch?v=qMVtUWH4Mx Y

A later update is here:
http://www.youtube.com/watch?v=d7DVfygOBlg &NR=1

This webpage outlines several of their key findings:
http://revealnow.com/key_findings.asp

Conclusion

At the time of this writing, we are not quite three years into our first steps in bringing the Church back home. This means we still have some kinks to work out, some questions to answer and some adjustments to make. However, the fact that not all our first steps have been smooth is okay with me because the fruit we have seen in the lives of those who are participating in Vineyard at Home has been astounding. There are three particular positive effects worth noting, thus far.

The first of these three is the defeat of the Pareto Principle; which is to say that we have enjoyed virtually 100% participation of all members of all ages in the life, mission and ministry of our Homegrown church. The sense of true discipleship - where the proverbial rubber meets the road - is inescapable.

I can only imagine how the experiences of our younger members will form and prepare them for a life of ongoing worship, service and outreach in the coming years. "Living church" (not just going to one) is already being woven in to their thinking, their values and their devotion to Christ and neighbor.

Adult members tell me again and again that they are experiencing unprecedented spiritual growth. This is true even in those cases where these believers have been active members of traditional congregations for many years. The level of ownership of the ministry and the "hands on" approach to everything from processing Scripture to organizing and accomplishing mission has simply put them in to a new personal growth arc when it comes to their faith development. This has been so exciting to watch in my own life as well as in the lives of my Vineyard at Home brothers and sisters in the Faith.

The second "payoff" – the big gem in all of this – has been to see the ministry of Jesus being taken *in reality* (and not just in theory) by everyday people to everyday places. Though an appetite for this was present in us from the beginning, to participate in the actual development and practice of this philosophy of ministry has been immensely gratifying. I'm truly excited to see where this ongoing quest will take us in the future.

And, finally, the third thing worth celebrating so far has been the way our resources have been maximized and distributed. We are already pretty lean and mean in the efficient utilization of our financial resources. I anticipate that this will become even more apparent as our Network grows. That's because our fixed expenses should remain a very low percentage of our overall budget even as the overall budget increases. Ultimately, the resources we will have available to spend on our mission should increase at a much faster rate than our fixed expenses. This is a dream come true.

This phenomenon of maximization of resources is also true when it comes to the employment of human resources. In all my years in church ministry, I have never seen a comparable quantity of actual ministry and outreach come from a church body or even a small group over a similar period of time. And, while this is true, the need for committees, outside meetings, and other time consuming interactions has been practically zero. We don't even plan our potlucks and yet (most of the time) the variety of food is astounding and we eat like princes and princesses. Go figure.

In sharing these observations I hope it is plain that I am not advocating that all believers must meet as we do or that our model is the one true template by which churches should measure their spiritual vitality or ecclesiastical legitimacy. I can legitimately report, however, that our first steps in bringing the Church back home have been most rewarding, truly energizing and – if they are indication of the future – a promising picture of things to come, if the Lord wills.

Made in the USA
Lexington, KY
29 January 2013